Love Letters to God

www.jilllowryministries.com

ISBN-13: 978-0-578-63390-9

Love Letters to God

Cover and Interior Design by Katharine E. Hamilton

Dedication

I am dedicating this book to my friends in Christ who have stood beside me,
prayed with me, and blessed my life in many ways.
I see Jesus in your eyes and love each of you dearly!

Introduction

Have you told God that you love Him lately? Have you written down your many blessings with a grateful heart? Many times we get so busy with the circumstances and problems of life that we forget to say thank you for our wonderful blessings. God loves a grateful heart, and He wants us to thank Him with a heart full of praise as we pray for what is on our heart.

King David wrote praises and prayers to God that are recorded in the Psalms. One prayer with praise is found in Psalm 86 titled "Great is Your Steadfast Love: A Prayer of David" Read his love letter to God and let your heart be full of promise!

"Incline your ear, O Lord, and answer me, for I am poor and needy. Preserve my life, for I am godly; save your servant, who trusts in you— you are my God. Be gracious to me, O Lord, for to you do I cry all the day. Gladden the soul of your servant, for to you, O Lord, do I lift up my soul. For you, O Lord, are good and forgiving, abounding in steadfast love to all who call upon you. Give ear, O Lord, to my prayer; listen to my plea for grace. In the day of trouble, I call upon you, for you answer me. There is none like you among the gods, O Lord, nor are there any works like yours. All the nations you have made shall come and worship before you, O Lord, and shall glorify your name. For you are great and do wondrous things; you alone are God. Teach me your way, O Lord, that I may walk in your truth; unite my heart to fear your name. I give thanks to you, O Lord, with my whole heart, and I will glorify your name forever."

Psalm 86:1-12

How do I use this gratitude journal?

Use this journal to write your love letters of praise and prayers to God, who is full of promise. Take a moment and read the praise, prayer, and promise from His Word and pour out your praises and prayers on the pages within. There is space on each page for you to write your love letters to God. As you write, you will discover that God's love will surround you and open your heart to a deeper relationship with Him. There's a place to date your letter, so that you can look back and see how your relationship with God has strengthened. Put down your troubles and pick up your pen as you pour out your heart to a loving God!

Blessings,

Jill Lowry

PRAISE

Thank God that He has brought you out of the darkness and into His great light and has given you His Holy Spirit if you choose to believe!

PRAYER

Pray that you will surrender all to Him and begin this year believing that you can live in the light with His freedom and power.

PROMISE

In Him was life, and the life was the light of men.
John 1:4

Write a love letter to God expressing your desire to grow closer to Him.

_____

_____

_____

_____

_____

_____

_____

_____

_____

Love Letter of Praise and Prayer

_____

_____

_____

_____

_____

_____

_____

_____

_____

_____

_____

_____

_____

_____

_____

_____

_____

_____

_____

_____

_____

_____

_____

_____

_____

_____

PRAISE

Thank God that the love of Jesus has made it possible for you to shine His light!

PRAYER

Pray that you will love with the love of Jesus by seeing with spiritual eyes.

PROMISE

Let your light shine before others, so that they may see your good works and give glory to your Father who is in heaven.
Matthew 5:16

Write a love letter to God expressing your desire to grow closer to Him.

_____

_____

_____

_____

_____

_____

_____

_____

_____

_____

Love Letter of Praise and Prayer

PRAISE

Thank God that Jesus Christ will give you more joy than you can ever dream or imagine!

PRAYER

Pray that you will trust Jesus by putting Him in the center of your life so that He can God-size your dreams and desires.

PROMISE

I wait for the Lord, my soul waits, and in his Word I hope.
Psalm 130:5

Write a love letter to God expressing your desire to grow closer to Him.

_____

_____

_____

_____

_____

_____

_____

_____

_____

_____

Love Letter of Praise and Prayer

_____

_____

_____

_____

_____

_____

_____

_____

_____

_____

_____

_____

_____

_____

_____

_____

_____

_____

_____

_____

_____

_____

_____

_____

_____

_____

PRAISE

Thank God that Jesus is your joy when you stay connected to His truth!

PRAYER

Pray that you will call upon the Lord in truth more intentionally and deeply so that you can find the pure joy that He desires for you.

PROMISE

The Lord is near to all who call upon Him, to all who call upon Him in truth.
Psalm 145:18

Write a love letter to God expressing your desire to grow closer to Him.

_____

_____

_____

_____

_____

_____

_____

_____

_____

_____

Love Letter of Praise and Prayer

_____

_____

_____

_____

_____

_____

_____

_____

_____

_____

_____

_____

_____

_____

_____

_____

_____

_____

_____

_____

_____

_____

_____

_____

_____

PRAISE

Thank God that Jesus heals you completely when you let Him comfort you with His love and cover you with His grace!

PRAYER

Pray that you will accept His love and grace, believing that He can and will heal you.

PROMISE

He heals the brokenhearted and binds up their wounds.
Psalm 147:3

Write a love letter to God expressing your desire to grow closer to Him.

_____

_____

_____

_____

_____

_____

_____

_____

_____

_____

Love Letter of Praise and Prayer

_____

_____

_____

_____

_____

_____

_____

_____

_____

_____

_____

_____

_____

_____

_____

_____

_____

_____

_____

_____

_____

_____

_____

_____

_____

PRAISE

Thank God that there is hope for an abundant life of blessings when we choose to follow Jesus to freedom!

PRAYER

Pray that you will trust God in all your ways because His ways are higher than your ways and His thoughts are higher than your thoughts.

PROMISE

How precious to me are your thoughts, O God! How vast is the sum of them!
Psalm 139:17

Write a love letter to God expressing your desire to grow closer to Him.

_____

_____

_____

_____

_____

_____

_____

_____

_____

_____

Love Letter of Praise and Prayer

_____

_____

_____

_____

_____

_____

_____

_____

_____

_____

_____

_____

_____

_____

_____

_____

_____

_____

_____

_____

_____

_____

Date: _____

PRAISE

Thank God that all who believe in Jesus, our living hope, will have salvation!

PRAYER

Pray that you will believe that you are forgiven and that you will do your part to spread the good news of hope that Jesus is our salvation.

PROMISE

For everyone who calls on the name of the Lord will be saved.
Romans 10:13

Write a love letter to God expressing your desire to grow closer to Him.

_____

_____

_____

_____

_____

_____

_____

_____

_____

_____

Love Letter of Praise and Prayer

_____
_____
_____
_____
_____
_____
_____
_____
_____
_____
_____
_____
_____
_____
_____
_____
_____
_____
_____
_____
_____
_____

PRAISE

Thank God for His perfect timing in your life as He know what you need even before you ask Him!

PRAYER

Pray that God will help you to be patient while waiting upon Him.

PROMISE

*The Lord is not slow to fulfill His promise as some count slowness,
but is patient towards you.*
2 Peter 3:9

Write a love letter to God expressing your desire to grow closer to Him.

_____

_____

_____

_____

_____

_____

_____

_____

_____

Love Letter of Praise and Prayer

_____
_____
_____
_____
_____
_____
_____
_____
_____
_____
_____
_____
_____
_____
_____
_____
_____
_____
_____
_____
_____
_____
_____
_____

PRAISE

Thank God for His answers to your prayers that you prayed in faith!

PRAYER

Pray in the Holy Spirit knowing that He intercedes for you
and takes your requests to the Father.

PROMISE

*But you, beloved, building yourselves up in your most Holy Faith
and praying in the Holy Spirit.*
Jude 1:20

Write a love letter to God expressing your desire to grow closer to Him.

_____

_____

_____

_____

_____

_____

_____

_____

_____

_____

Love Letter of Praise and Prayer

_____

_____

_____

_____

_____

_____

_____

_____

_____

_____

_____

_____

_____

_____

_____

_____

_____

_____

_____

_____

_____

_____

_____

_____

_____

PRAISE

Thank God that the love and power from the Spirit
refreshes, restores, renews and revives you!

PRAYER

Pray that you will make Jesus the first love of your life so that you can be rejuvenated.

PROMISE

So now faith, hope, and love abide, these three, but the greatest of these is love.
1 Corinthians 13:13

Write a love letter to God expressing your desire to grow closer to Him.

_____
_____
_____
_____
_____
_____
_____
_____
_____
_____

Love Letter of Praise and Prayer

_____

_____

_____

_____

_____

_____

_____

_____

_____

_____

_____

_____

_____

_____

_____

_____

_____

_____

_____

_____

_____

_____

_____

_____

_____

_____

Date: _____

PRAISE
Thank God that He lavishes you with His amazing grace
so that you can have freedom and hope!

PRAYER
Pray that you can keep following Jesus one step at a time
even when you do not see all the details.

PROMISE
Follow me.
John 21:19

Write a love letter to God expressing your desire to grow closer to Him.

_____

_____

_____

_____

_____

_____

_____

_____

_____

_____

Love Letter of Praise and Prayer

_____

_____

_____

_____

_____

_____

_____

_____

_____

_____

_____

_____

_____

_____

_____

_____

_____

_____

_____

_____

_____

_____

_____

_____

_____

_____

_____

PRAISE
Thank God that He hears us when we pray and is among us as we pray in one accord!

PRAYER
Pray that you will make every effort to pray faithfully in one accord with others.

PROMISE
All these with one accord were devoting themselves to prayer.
Acts 1:14

Write a love letter to God expressing your desire to grow closer to Him.

_____

_____

_____

_____

_____

_____

_____

_____

_____

_____

_____

_____

Love Letter of Praise and Prayer

_____
_____
_____
_____
_____
_____
_____
_____
_____
_____
_____
_____
_____
_____
_____
_____
_____
_____
_____
_____
_____
_____
_____
_____
_____

Date: _____

PRAISE
Thank God that He remains faithful and will do what He promises!

PRAYER
Pray that you will keep being faithful because He is always faithful to you.

PROMISE
He who calls you is faithful; He will surely do it.
1 Thessalonians 5:24

Write a love letter to God expressing your desire to grow closer to Him.

_____

_____

_____

_____

_____

_____

_____

_____

_____

_____

_____

_____

Love Letter of Praise and Prayer

_____
_____
_____
_____
_____
_____
_____
_____
_____
_____
_____
_____
_____
_____
_____
_____
_____
_____
_____
_____
_____
_____
_____
_____
_____
_____
_____

PRAISE

Thank God that He will meet every need of yours
and supply you with the riches of His Kingdom!

PRAYER

Pray that you will continue working faithfully for the Lord in harmony
with one another as He has called you.

PROMISE

Your faith is growing abundantly,
and the love of every one of you for another is increasing.
2 Thessalonians 1:3

Write a love letter to God expressing your desire to grow closer to Him.

_____

_____

_____

_____

_____

_____

_____

_____

_____

Love Letter of Praise and Prayer

_____
_____
_____
_____
_____
_____
_____
_____
_____
_____
_____
_____
_____
_____
_____
_____
_____
_____
_____
_____
_____
_____
_____

PRAISE

Thank God that you were created to be renewed in your mind through
the love of Jesus Christ!

PRAYER

Pray that you can have a surrendered heart and a renewed mind.

PROMISE

Do not be conformed to this world, but be transformed by the renewal of your mind.
Romans 12:2

Write a love letter to God expressing your desire to grow closer to Him.

_____

_____

_____

_____

_____

_____

_____

_____

_____

_____

Love Letter of Praise and Prayer

_____

_____

_____

_____

_____

_____

_____

_____

_____

_____

_____

_____

_____

_____

_____

_____

_____

_____

_____

_____

_____

_____

_____

_____

PRAISE
Thank God for His strength and power in your life!

PRAYER
Pray that you will put God in the center and let Him use you as a vessel for His glory.

PROMISE
The Lord stood by me and strengthened me.
2 Timothy 4:7

Write a love letter to God expressing your desire to grow closer to Him.

_____

_____

_____

_____

_____

_____

_____

_____

_____

_____

_____

Love Letter of Praise and Prayer

_____
_____
_____
_____
_____
_____
_____
_____
_____
_____
_____
_____
_____
_____
_____
_____
_____
_____
_____
_____
_____
_____
_____
_____
_____

Date: _____

PRAISE

Thank God that He is your perfect peace and will give you a life of promise!

PRAYER

Pray that you will trust the Lord with your whole heart
so that His perfect peace can enter your heart.

PROMISE

You keep him in perfect peace whose mind is stayed on you, because He trusts in you.
Isaiah 26:3

Write a love letter to God expressing your desire to grow closer to Him.

_____

_____

_____

_____

_____

_____

_____

_____

_____

_____

Love Letter of Praise and Prayer

_____
_____
_____
_____
_____
_____
_____
_____
_____
_____
_____
_____
_____
_____
_____
_____
_____
_____
_____
_____
_____
_____
_____
_____

PRAISE

Thank God that His word remains true and never fails!

PRAYER

Pray that you will find more time to spend in His word so that you can experience a deeper relationship with Jesus as you focus on His truth.

PROMISE

The grass withers, the flower falls, but the word of the Lord remains forever.
1 Peter 1:24-25

Write a love letter to God expressing your desire to grow closer to Him.

_____

_____

_____

_____

_____

_____

_____

_____

_____

_____

Love Letter of Praise and Prayer

_____
_____
_____
_____
_____
_____
_____
_____
_____
_____
_____
_____
_____
_____
_____
_____
_____
_____
_____
_____
_____
_____
_____
_____

Date: _____

PRAISE

Thank God that He is doing a new thing in your life!

PRAYER

Pray that you will find new life as you put Christ in the center.

PROMISE

Behold, he is doing a new thing; now it springs forth, do you not perceive it?
Isaiah 43:19

Write a love letter to God expressing your desire to grow closer to Him.

_____

_____

_____

_____

_____

_____

_____

_____

_____

_____

_____

_____

_____

Love Letter of Praise and Prayer

_____

_____

_____

_____

_____

_____

_____

_____

_____

_____

_____

_____

_____

_____

_____

_____

_____

_____

_____

_____

_____

_____

_____

_____

PRAISE

Thank God that He will take away all your worries and your fears because He cares for you!

PRAYER

Pray that you will turn up the volume of His Spirit
and breathe out the peace of Christ into your life.

PROMISE

Cast all your anxieties on Him, because He cares for you.
1 Peter 5:7

Write a love letter to God expressing your desire to grow closer to Him.

_____

_____

_____

_____

_____

_____

_____

_____

_____

_____

Love Letter of Praise and Prayer

PRAISE

Thank God that He shows Himself to you in mighty ways!

PRAYER

Pray that you will let Jesus touch you with His healing and wholeness
to give you new life.

PROMISE

Blessed are the pure in heart, for they shall see God.
Matthew 5:8

Write a love letter to God expressing your desire to grow closer to Him.

_____

_____

_____

_____

_____

_____

_____

_____

_____

_____

_____

Love Letter of Praise and Prayer

_____
_____
_____
_____
_____
_____
_____
_____
_____
_____
_____
_____
_____
_____
_____
_____
_____
_____
_____
_____
_____
_____
_____
_____
_____

PRAISE

Thank God that you have a friend in Jesus who will never let you down!

PRAYER

Pray that you can forgive the ones who have come against you
and that you can love in truth and deed.

PROMISE

Little children, let us not love in word or talk, but in deed and truth.
1 John 3:18

Write a love letter to God expressing your desire to grow closer to Him.

_____

_____

_____

_____

_____

_____

_____

_____

_____

_____

Love Letter of Praise and Prayer

_____
_____
_____
_____
_____
_____
_____
_____
_____
_____
_____
_____
_____
_____
_____
_____
_____
_____
_____
_____
_____
_____
_____
_____
_____
_____

Date: _____

PRAISE
Thank God that Jesus came to give you abundant life!

PRAYER
Pray that you will give Jesus your whole heart
so that He can fill all your days with His joy.

PROMISE
Jesus came that you may have life and have it abundantly.
John 10:10

Write a love letter to God expressing your desire to grow closer to Him.

_____

_____

_____

_____

_____

_____

_____

_____

_____

_____

Love Letter of Praise and Prayer

PRAISE

Thank God that Jesus can and will break down the walls that divide us!

PRAYER

Pray that you will make every effort to live in harmony with your neighbor so that you can experience unity through Jesus Christ.

PROMISE

For He Himself is our peace, who had made us both one and has broken down in His flesh the dividing wall of hostility.
Ephesians 2:14

Write a love letter to God expressing your desire to grow closer to Him.

_____

_____

_____

_____

_____

_____

_____

_____

_____

_____

Love Letter of Praise and Prayer

PRAISE

Thank God that you can be free in Christ when you step out in faith!

PRAYER

Pray that you will listen to the whisper of the voice of God
and grab hold of the life that He wants to give you.

PROMISE

For freedom Christ has set us free.
Galatians 5:1

Write a love letter to God expressing your desire to grow closer to Him.

_____

_____

_____

_____

_____

_____

_____

_____

_____

_____

Love Letter of Praise and Prayer

_____

_____

_____

_____

_____

_____

_____

_____

_____

_____

_____

_____

_____

_____

_____

_____

_____

_____

_____

_____

_____

_____

_____

_____

_____

_____

_____

_____

PRAISE

Thank God that He will show you amazing things when you choose to follow, trust, and obey Him with your whole heart!

PRAYER

Pray that you can open your heart to the Lord and let His love overwhelm you and His peace transform you.

PROMISE

I will give them a new heart, to know that I am the Lord, and they shall be my people and I shall be their God, for they shall return to me with their whole heart.
Jeremiah 24:7

Write a love letter to God expressing your desire to grow closer to Him.

_____

_____

_____

_____

_____

_____

_____

_____

_____

Love Letter of Praise and Prayer

Date: _____

PRAISE

Thank God you are new and alive in Christ and can see with your spiritual eyes!

PRAYER

Pray that you will let God show you the divine purpose that He has for you
as you keep your eyes fixed on Jesus.

PROMISE

Blessed are your eyes, for they see, and your ears, for they hear.
Matthew 13:16

Write a love letter to God expressing your desire to grow closer to Him.

_____

_____

_____

_____

_____

_____

_____

_____

_____

_____

Love Letter of Praise and Prayer

_____

_____

_____

_____

_____

_____

_____

_____

_____

_____

_____

_____

_____

_____

_____

_____

_____

_____

_____

_____

_____

_____

_____

_____

_____

_____

_____

PRAISE

Thank God that He hears you when you pray by pouring your heart out to Him!

PRAYER

Pray that you will keep asking, seeking, and knocking so that the Lord can answer your faithful, brave, and bold prayers.

PROMISE

Ask and it will be given to you; seek, and you will find; knock, and the door will be opened to you.
Matthew 7:7

Write a love letter to God expressing your desire to grow closer to Him.

_____

_____

_____

_____

_____

_____

_____

_____

_____

_____

Love Letter of Praise and Prayer

_____
_____
_____
_____
_____
_____
_____
_____
_____
_____
_____
_____
_____
_____
_____
_____
_____
_____
_____
_____
_____
_____
_____
_____
_____
_____
_____

Date: _____

PRAISE

Thank God that He will awaken you with new life as you come out of the darkness and into His great light!

PRAYER

Pray that you will let the peace of Christ cover you, so that you can feel the power of His love and the hope of His light in a brand new way.

PROMISE

God is light, and in Him is no darkness at all.
1 John 1:5

Write a love letter to God expressing your desire to grow closer to Him.

_____

_____

_____

_____

_____

_____

_____

_____

_____

Love Letter of Praise and Prayer

_____

_____

_____

_____

_____

_____

_____

_____

_____

_____

_____

_____

_____

_____

_____

_____

_____

_____

_____

_____

_____

_____

_____

_____

PRAISE

Thank God that you can live with endurance and strength
when you wait upon the Lord to renew you!

PRAYER

Pray that you will take off your old self and let God make you new,
so that you can rise up with new wings.

PROMISE

They who wait upon the Lord shall renew their strength;
they shall mount up with wings like eagles; they shall run and not be weary;
they shall walk and not faint.
Isaiah 40:31

Write a love letter to God expressing your desire to grow closer to Him.

_____

_____

_____

_____

_____

_____

_____

Love Letter of Praise and Prayer

_____
_____
_____
_____
_____
_____
_____
_____
_____
_____
_____
_____
_____
_____
_____
_____
_____
_____
_____
_____
_____
_____
_____

Date: _____

PRAISE

Thank God that you have been saved by His great grace
and that you can experience hope and salvation through grace!

PRAYER

Pray that you will not be afraid to trust God and accept His grace
so that you can see others with spiritual eyes of grace.

PROMISE

Behold, God is my salvation; I will trust, and will not be afraid.
Isaiah 12:2

Write a love letter to God expressing your desire to grow closer to Him.

_____

_____

_____

_____

_____

_____

_____

_____

_____

_____

Love Letter of Praise and Prayer

_____

_____

_____

_____

_____

_____

_____

_____

_____

_____

_____

_____

_____

_____

_____

_____

_____

_____

_____

_____

_____

_____

_____

_____

PRAISE
Thank God that His love remains true and that He will never fail you!

PRAYER
Pray that you will call upon His counsel and seek the Lord with all your heart.

PROMISE
You shall love the Lord your God with all your heart,
with all your soul, and with all your might.
Deuteronomy 6:5

Write a love letter to God expressing your desire to grow closer to Him.

_____

_____

_____

_____

_____

_____

_____

_____

_____

_____

Love Letter of Praise and Prayer

PRAISE

Thank God that He has taken away all your fears and has given you a spirit of power, love, and self-control!

PRAYER

Pray that you will stop fearing and start trusting Jesus in all that you do.

PROMISE

God gave us not a spirit of fear, but of power, and love, and self-control.
2 Timothy 1:7

Write a love letter to God expressing your desire to grow closer to Him.

_____

_____

_____

_____

_____

_____

_____

_____

_____

_____

_____

Love Letter of Praise and Prayer

_____

_____

_____

_____

_____

_____

_____

_____

_____

_____

_____

_____

_____

_____

_____

_____

_____

_____

_____

_____

_____

_____

_____

PRAISE

Thank God that He loved you so much that He gave you
eternal hope and peace through Jesus Christ!

PRAYER

Pray that you will surrender all to the one who surrendered all for you on Calvary.

PROMISE

Therefore, since we have been justified by faith,
we have peace with God through our Lord Jesus Christ.
Romans 5:1

Write a love letter to God expressing your desire to grow closer to Him.

_____

_____

_____

_____

_____

_____

_____

_____

_____

_____

Love Letter of Praise and Prayer

_____
_____
_____
_____
_____
_____
_____
_____
_____
_____
_____
_____
_____
_____
_____
_____
_____
_____
_____
_____
_____
_____
_____
_____

Date: _____

PRAISE

Thank God that the Lord is always faithful to you!

PRAYER

Pray that you will faithfully serve where He calls you and follow where He leads you.

PROMISE

For not all have faith, but the Lord is faithful.
2 Thessalonians 3:2-3

Write a love letter to God expressing your desire to grow closer to Him.

_____
_____
_____
_____
_____
_____
_____
_____
_____
_____
_____

Love Letter of Praise and Prayer

_____

_____

_____

_____

_____

_____

_____

_____

_____

_____

_____

_____

_____

_____

_____

_____

_____

_____

_____

_____

_____

_____

_____

_____

Date: _____

PRAISE
Thank God that He is a God of second chances!

PRAYER
Pray that you will stay connected to the Lord and let His grace cover you completely.

PROMISE
To set the mind on the flesh is death, but to set the mind on the Spirit is life and peace.
Romans 8:6

Write a love letter to God expressing your desire to grow closer to Him.

_____

_____

_____

_____

_____

_____

_____

_____

_____

_____

_____

Love Letter of Praise and Prayer

Date: _____

PRAISE

Thank God that He will be your rock and refuge in any storm you face!

PRAYER

Pray that you will abide in the love of Jesus and walk in the way in which He walked.

PROMISE

Whoever says he abides in Him ought to walk in the same way in which He walked.
1 John 2:6

Write a love letter to God expressing your desire to grow closer to Him.

_____

_____

_____

_____

_____

_____

_____

_____

_____

_____

_____

_____

Love Letter of Praise and Prayer

_____

_____

_____

_____

_____

_____

_____

_____

_____

_____

_____

_____

_____

_____

_____

_____

_____

_____

_____

_____

_____

_____

_____

_____

_____

_____

_____

_____

PRAISE

Thank God that you know the truth that He who is in you is greater than
He who lives in the world!

PRAYER

Pray that you will let the Spirit lead you into all truth.

PROMISE

He who is in you is greater than he who is in the world.
1 John 4:4

Write a love letter to God expressing your desire to grow closer to Him.

_____

_____

_____

_____

_____

_____

_____

_____

_____

_____

Love Letter of Praise and Prayer

_____
_____
_____
_____
_____
_____
_____
_____
_____
_____
_____
_____
_____
_____
_____
_____
_____
_____
_____
_____
_____
_____
_____
_____
_____
_____
_____

PRAISE

Thank God that He is the Shepherd and Overseer of your soul!

PRAYER

Pray that you will come back to your Shepherd and let Him lead you and protect you.

PROMISE

But you were straying like sheep, but now have returned to the Shepherd and Overseer of your souls.
1 Peter 2:25

Write a love letter to God expressing your desire to grow closer to Him.

_____

_____

_____

_____

_____

_____

_____

_____

_____

_____

Love Letter of Praise and Prayer

_____
_____
_____
_____
_____
_____
_____
_____
_____
_____
_____
_____
_____
_____
_____
_____
_____
_____
_____
_____
_____
_____
_____
_____
_____
_____
_____
_____
_____
_____
_____
_____
_____

PRAISE

Thank God that His gospel message is alive and brings hope to all who believe!

PRAYER

Pray that you will be faithful to the Lord by trusting and obeying His word of truth.

PROMISE

For we are not ashamed of the gospel, for it is the power of God for salvation to everyone who believes.
Romans 1:16

Write a love letter to God expressing your desire to grow closer to Him.

_____

_____

_____

_____

_____

_____

_____

_____

_____

Love Letter of Praise and Prayer

PRAISE

Thank God that He will continue to strengthen you
and bring you through the fire by igniting a Holy Fire in you!

PRAYER

Pray that you will live moment by moment,
setting your mind on the things above that come from the Lord.

PROMISE

I can do all things through Him who strengthens me.
Philippians 4:13

Write a love letter to God expressing your desire to grow closer to Him.

_____

_____

_____

_____

_____

_____

_____

_____

_____

_____

Love Letter of Praise and Prayer

_____
_____
_____
_____
_____
_____
_____
_____
_____
_____
_____
_____
_____
_____
_____
_____
_____
_____
_____
_____
_____
_____
_____
_____
_____
_____
_____
_____
_____
_____
_____

PRAISE
Thank God that His word gives you life and power!

PRAYER
Pray that you will live connected to His Spirit of truth and love.

PROMISE
All Scripture is breathed out by God.
2 Timothy 3:16

Write a love letter to God expressing your desire to grow closer to Him.

_____

_____

_____

_____

_____

_____

_____

_____

_____

_____

_____

_____

Love Letter of Praise and Prayer

_____

_____

_____

_____

_____

_____

_____

_____

_____

_____

_____

_____

_____

_____

_____

_____

_____

_____

_____

_____

_____

_____

_____

_____

PRAISE

Thank God that His perfect love casts out fear and that His grace brings salvation for all!

PRAYER

Pray that you will let His Spirit of freedom and truth come alive in you.

PROMISE

For the grace of God has appeared, bringing salvation for all people.
Titus 2:11

Write a love letter to God expressing your desire to grow closer to Him.

_____
_____
_____
_____
_____
_____
_____
_____
_____
_____
_____

Love Letter of Praise and Prayer

_____

_____

_____

_____

_____

_____

_____

_____

_____

_____

_____

_____

_____

_____

_____

_____

_____

_____

_____

_____

_____

_____

_____

_____

_____

_____

_____

_____

PRAISE

Thank God that the power source of Jesus will fill you up and refresh you!

PRAYER

Pray that you will turn to Jesus and let go of everything that hinders you.

PROMISE

For He will come like a rushing stream, which the wind of the Lord drives.
Isaiah 59:19

Write a love letter to God expressing your desire to grow closer to Him.

_____

_____

_____

_____

_____

_____

_____

_____

_____

_____

_____

_____

Love Letter of Praise and Prayer

_____

_____

_____

_____

_____

_____

_____

_____

_____

_____

_____

_____

_____

_____

_____

_____

_____

_____

_____

_____

_____

_____

_____

_____

_____

_____

PRAISE

Thank God that He grows much fruit in you as you keep abiding in His great love for you!

PRAYER

Pray that you will continue abiding in Him
by staying connected to Jesus, your power source.

PROMISE

As the Father has loved me, so have I loved you. Abide in my love.
John 15:9

Write a love letter to God expressing your desire to grow closer to Him.

_____

_____

_____

_____

_____

_____

_____

_____

_____

_____

Love Letter of Praise and Prayer

_____

_____

_____

_____

_____

_____

_____

_____

_____

_____

_____

_____

_____

_____

_____

_____

_____

_____

_____

_____

_____

_____

PRAISE
Thank God that He is ready to bless you with many blessings of great joy!

PRAYER
Pray that you would be able to pray your boldest prayers believing, that you will receive.

PROMISE
Until now you have asked nothing in my name.
Ask and you will receive that your joy may be full.
John 16:24

Write a love letter to God expressing your desire to grow closer to Him.

_____

_____

_____

_____

_____

_____

_____

_____

_____

_____

Love Letter of Praise and Prayer

_____
_____
_____
_____
_____
_____
_____
_____
_____
_____
_____
_____
_____
_____
_____
_____
_____
_____
_____
_____
_____
_____
_____
_____
_____

PRAISE

Thank God for His gift of the Holy Spirit who is the same Spirit that lives in Jesus!

PRAYER

Pray that you will receive the Holy Spirit and listen to His voice.

PROMISE

Receive the Holy Spirit.
John 20:22

Write a love letter to God expressing your desire to grow closer to Him.

_____

_____

_____

_____

_____

_____

_____

_____

_____

_____

_____

Love Letter of Praise and Prayer

_____

_____

_____

_____

_____

_____

_____

_____

_____

_____

_____

_____

_____

_____

_____

_____

_____

_____

_____

_____

_____

_____

_____

_____

_____

Date: _____

PRAISE

Thank God that He shows His glory to those who believe!

PRAYER

Pray that you will believe and let your faith take to a higher place with Jesus today.

PROMISE

Jesus said to her, "Did I not tell you that if you believed you would see the glory of God?"
John 11:40

Write a love letter to God expressing your desire to grow closer to Him.

_____

_____

_____

_____

_____

_____

_____

_____

_____

_____

_____

Love Letter of Praise and Prayer

_____

_____

_____

_____

_____

_____

_____

_____

_____

_____

_____

_____

_____

_____

_____

_____

_____

_____

_____

_____

_____

_____

_____

_____

Do you want to ignite a spark in your heart for Jesus?

Psalm 16:11 says that "In the presence of Jesus there is fullness of joy and at His right hand are pleasures forevermore."

To set your heart on fire for Jesus, you need to open your heart to His love and spend time with Him in His word and prayer. Spend time "with Jesus" as you read this daily devotional of encouragement and truth from scriptures in the Bible.

Each day you will be enlightened to another treasure from His word that He wants to share with you. Sit at His feet and listen to His voice calling you to a deeper relationship with Him. Turn to the only true light of the world, Jesus Christ. He is waiting for you to spend time "with Him" so that He can ignite a fire in your heart!

Are you searching for more joy?

Do you believe that you can find joy?

Discover that joy is possible through Jesus!

Jill Lowry shares fifty-two inspiring devotionals partnered with beautiful color photographs and scriptures to encourage your heart. As you read these heart-felt devotions, may the love of Jesus fall upon you and fill you with abundant and overflowing joy.

About the Author

Jill Lowry is an ardent follower of Jesus who has a desire and passion to communicate His truth. Her writings combine the accuracy of a scholar with the practicality of a wife and mother. Jill grew up in San Antonio, Texas. She graduated from the University of Texas with a Bachelor of Business Administration in Marketing and holds a law degree from St. Mary's University in San Antonio.

Her ministries include helping mentor and feed at-risk students, co-leading a women's bible study, co-hosting a weekly radio show that answers questions of faith, and praying with fellow believers in a weekly community prayer group.

Jill is the founder and president of a student mentoring and food program, Mt Vernon Cares, created for at-risk students at the local Junior High and High School. She is also one of the hosts of a faith-based weekly radio talk show and podcast, Real Life Real People Radio.

http://www.realliferealpeopleradio.podbean.com

Jill takes every opportunity to pray with friends and neighbors in need and considers intercessory prayer a vital part of her ministry. She is part of a weekly community prayer group which meets on the Downtown Square to pray for revival in her community and beyond. Visit her website and subscribe to receive daily prayers.

http://www.jilllowryministries.com

Made in the USA
Monee, IL
23 February 2020